We hope you enjoy coloring this book.

Download some extra

free coloring patterns

and get news of upcoming books at

www.scribblepresscoloring.com/free-download

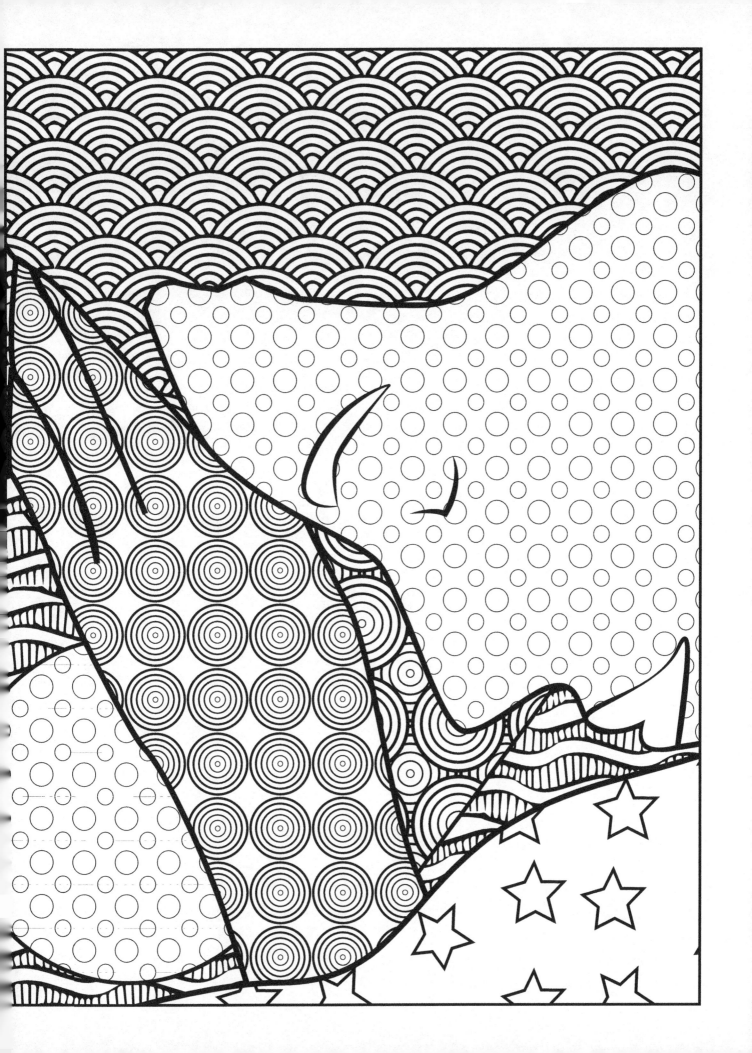

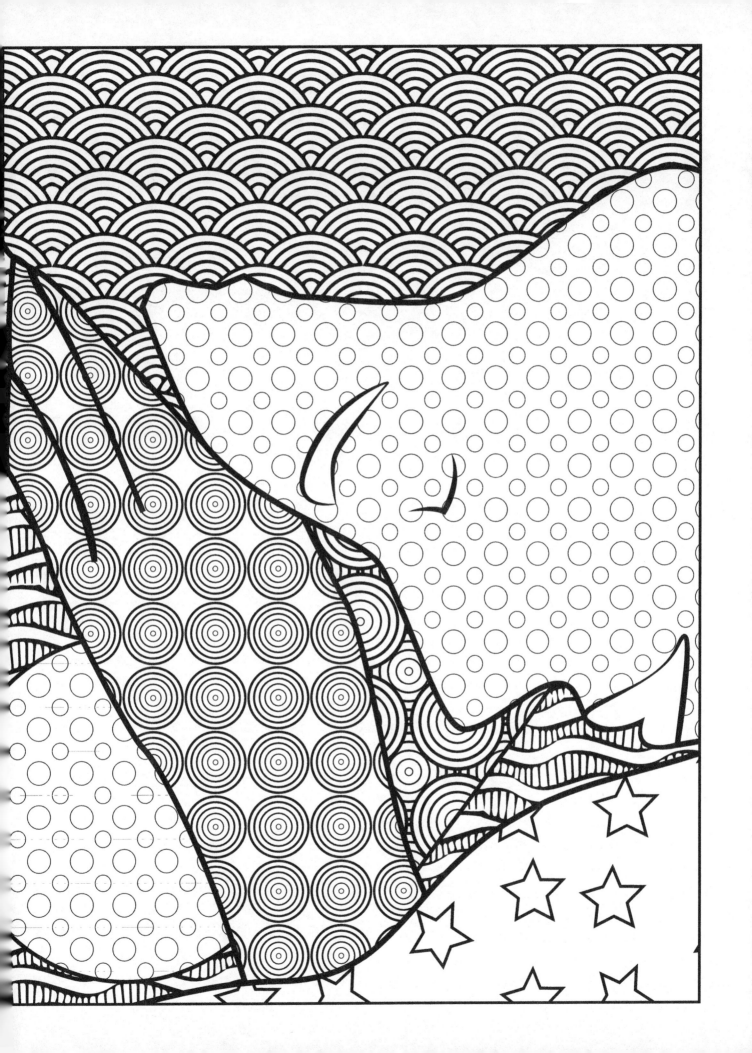

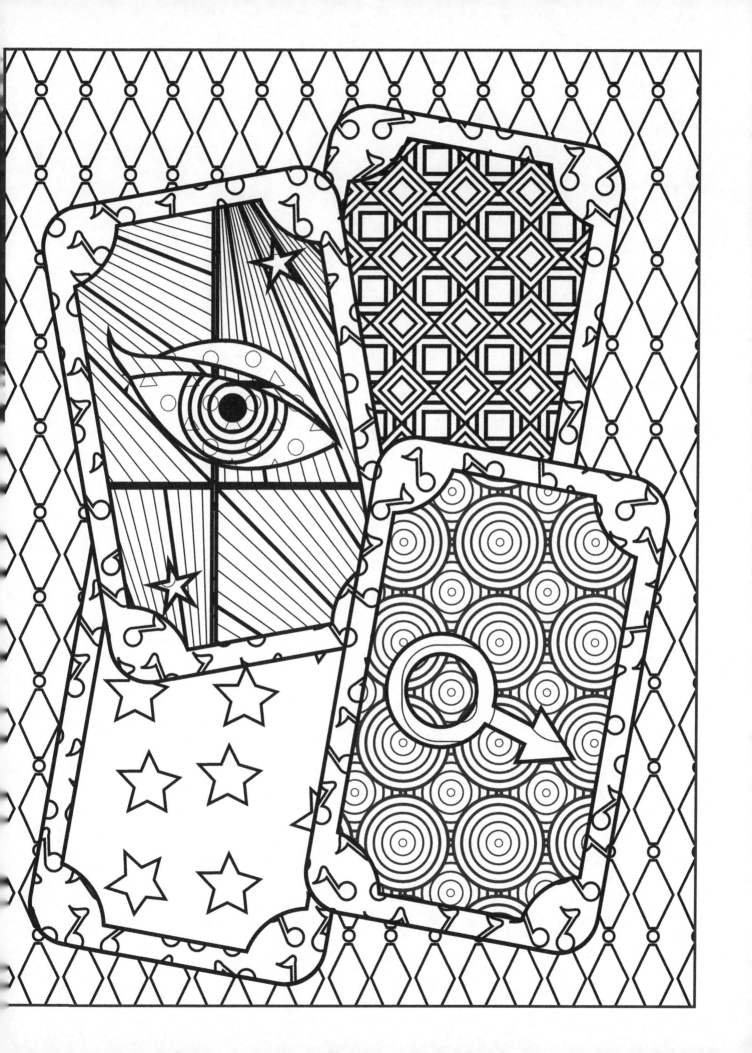

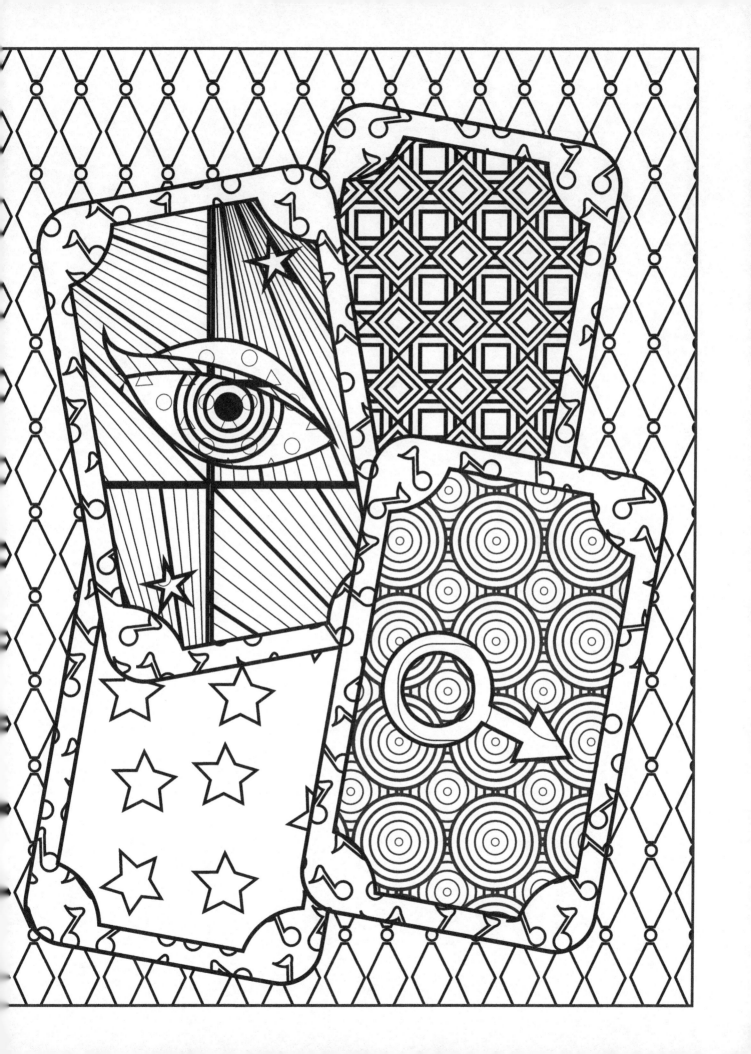

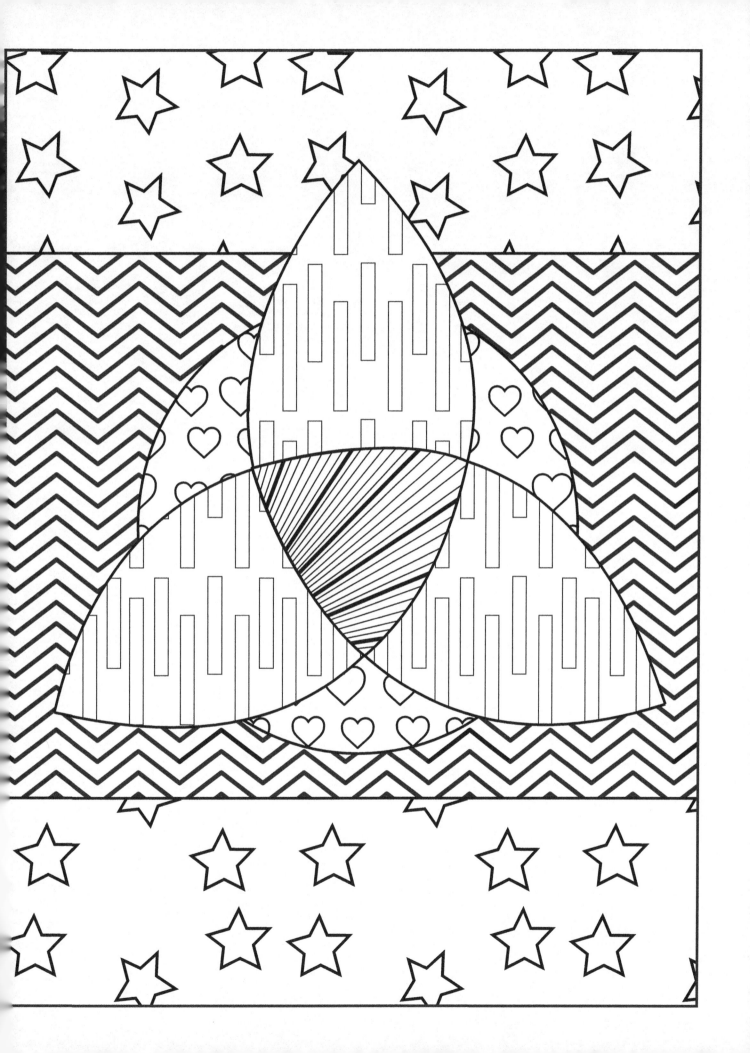

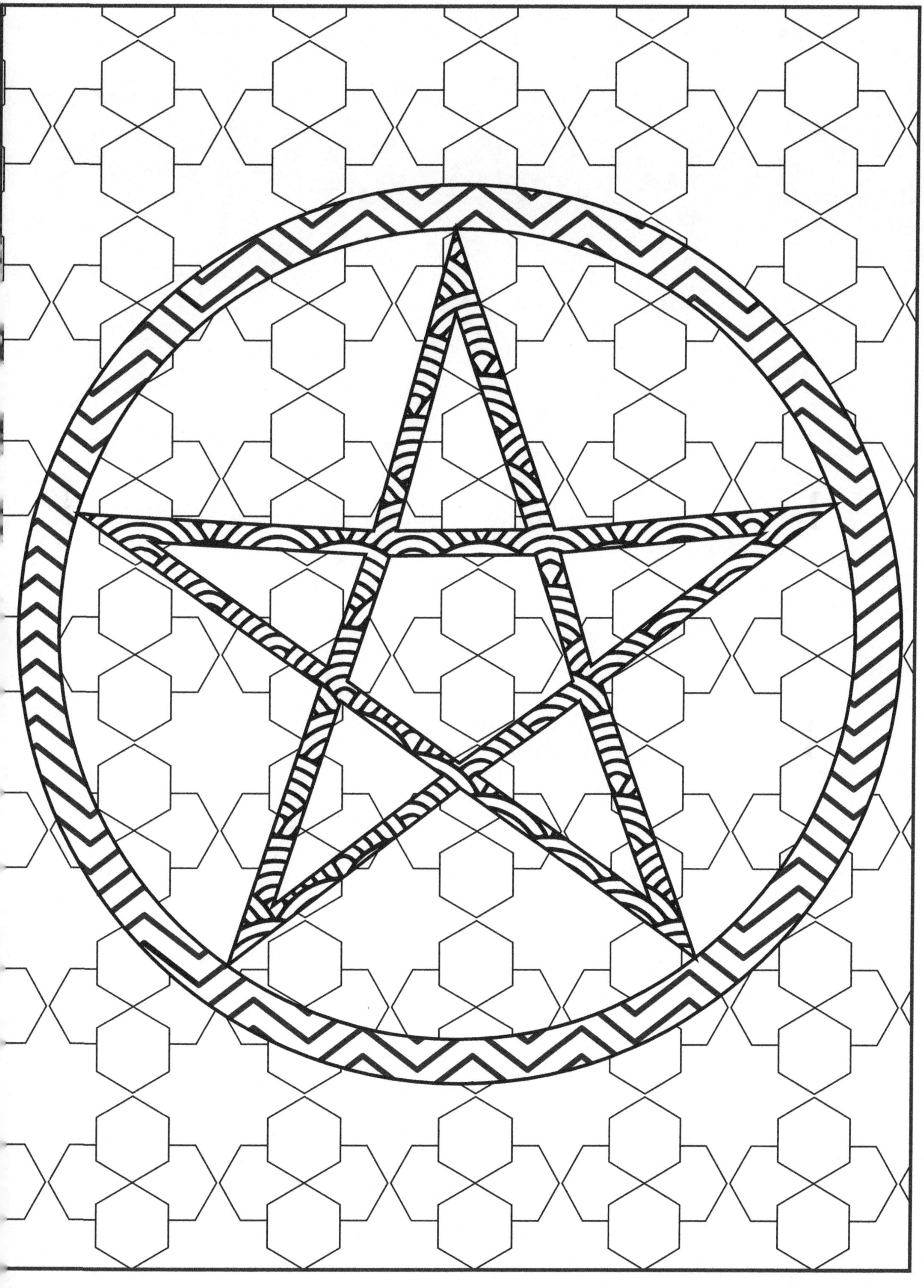

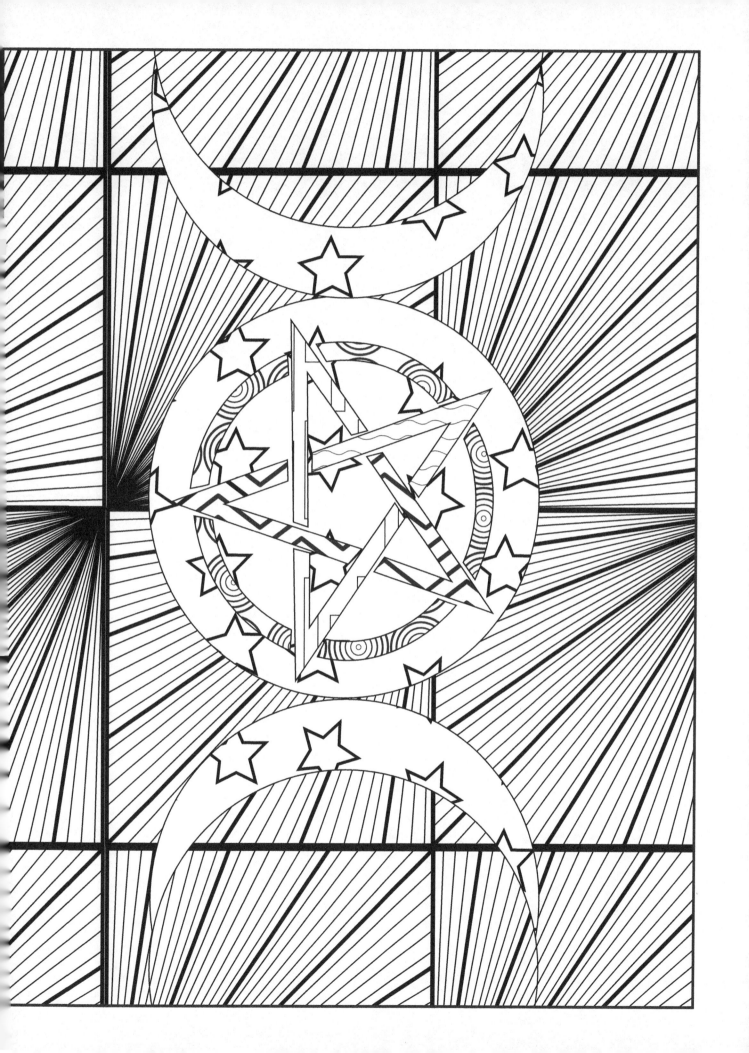

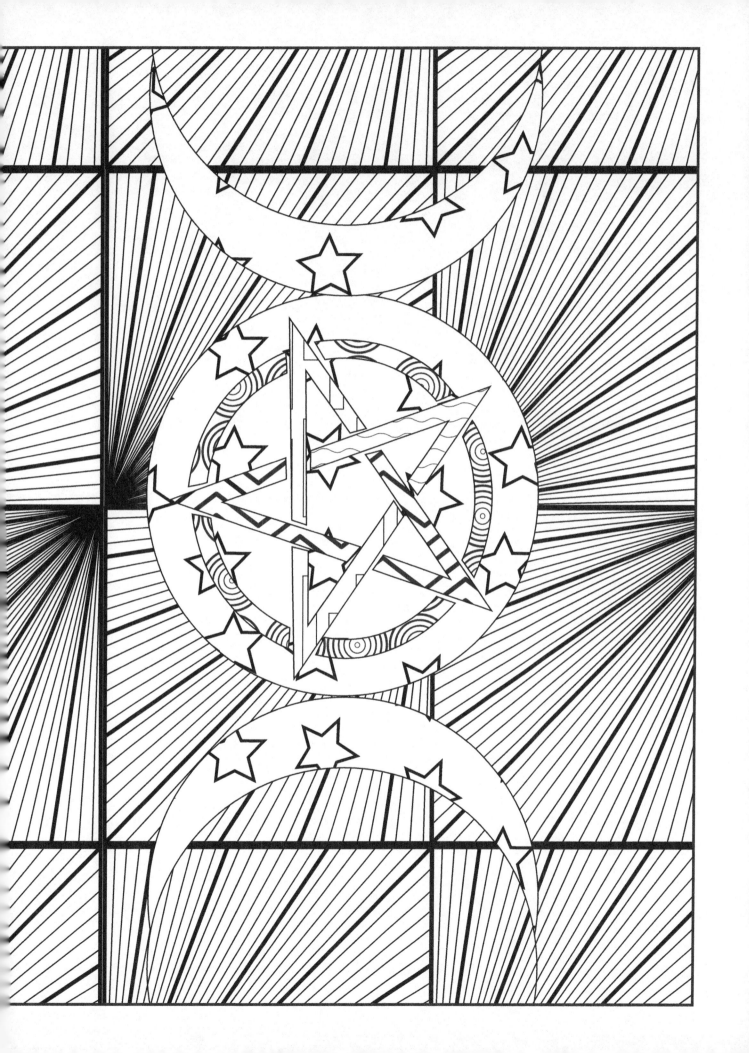

Made in the USA
Monee, IL
15 December 2023

49498878R00070